Angela Porter's
TROPICAL RAINFOREST
HIDDEN PICTURES

Forever Inspired COLORING BOOK

Angela Porter's
TROPICAL RAINFOREST
HIDDEN PICTURES

ANGELA PORTER

FOR YOUNG READERS

Find these hidden pictures throughout the following illustrations!

Tropical Rainforests

Ladybugs		59
Snails		9
Hearts		150
Stars		108

HIDDEN PICTURE
ANSWER KEY

1

2

3

4

5

6

7

8

9

10

11

12

13

14

15

16

17

18

19

20

21

22

23

24

25

26

27

28

29

30

31

32

33

34

35

PALETTE BARS

Use these bars to test your coloring medium and palette. Don't be afraid to try unique color combinations!